I0605277

Made with love by the team at

FIVE MILE

Five Mile,
the publishing division
of Regency Media
www.fivemile.com.au

Printed in China 5 4 3 2 1

A catalogue record for this book is available from the National Library of Australia

EXPLORE NATURE

Search and Find

CANYON

Hidden in the canyon can you find...

3 Rattlesnakes

4 Bald Eagles

5 Ringtails

6 Canyon Wrens

How many animals can you see?

What was your favorite animal on this page?

Have you ever been to the Grand Canyon?

WETLAND

In the wetlands can you find...

1 Blue Heron

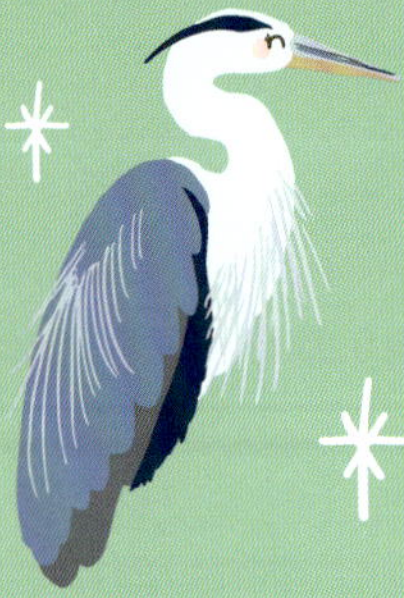

2 Alligators

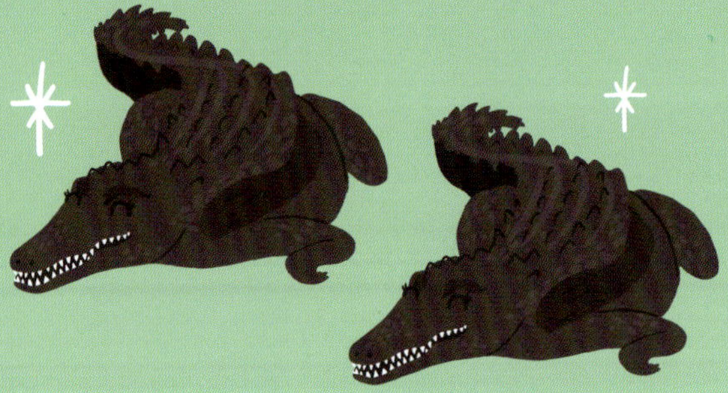

3 Turtles

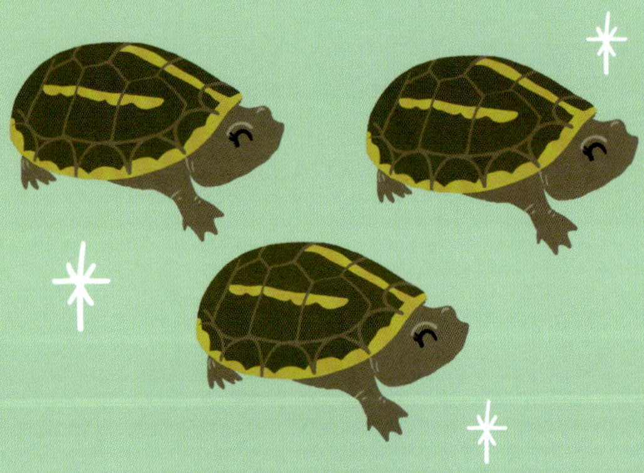

4 Bromeliads

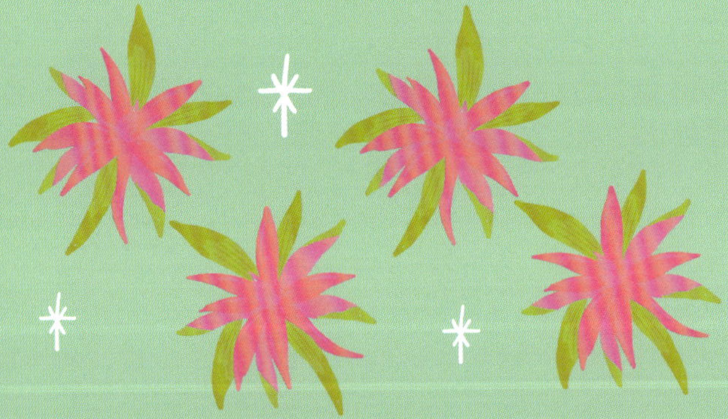

5 Frogs

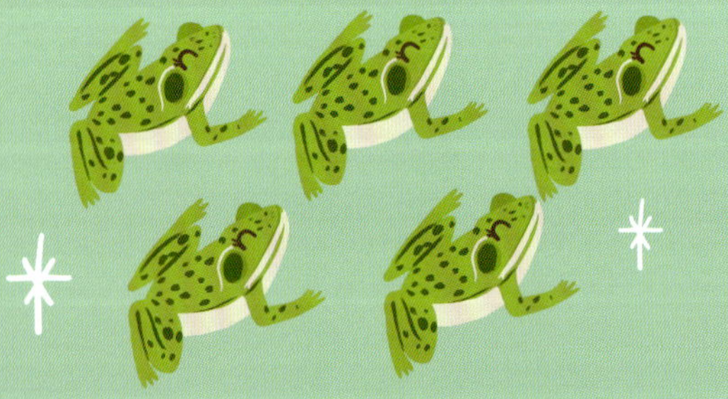

6 Yellow Water Lilies

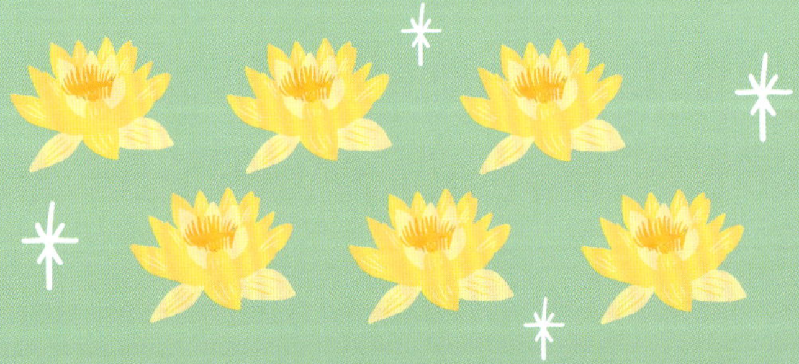

How many creatures are near the water?

What was your favorite thing on this page?

Have you ever been to the Everglades?

PRAIRIE

In the sunny fields can you find...

1 Rattlesnake

2 Coyotes

3 Burrowing Owls

4 Prairie Dogs

5 Bison

6 Monarch Butterflies

EXTRAS!

How many flowers can you see?

What was your favorite thing on this page?

Have you seen a Prairie before?

WATERFALL

By the waterfall can you find...

1 American Robin

2 Coyotes

3 Skunks

4 Black Bears

5 Acorn Woodpeckers

6 Grasshoppers

EXTRAS!

Have you seen a skunk before?

Where did you see it?

What's the biggest waterfall you've ever seen?

FOREST

Hiding in the forest can you find..

1 Black Bear

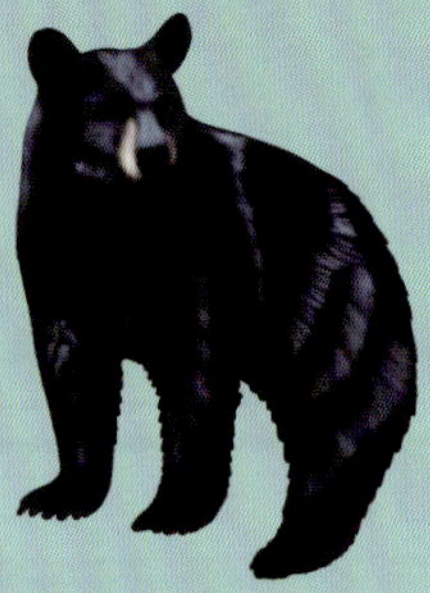

2 Elk

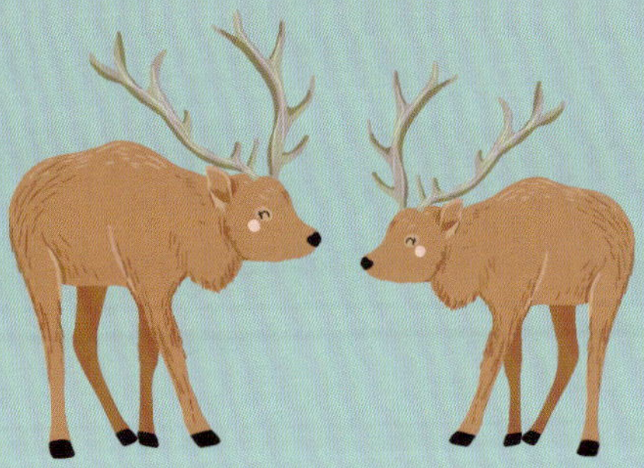

3 Squirrels

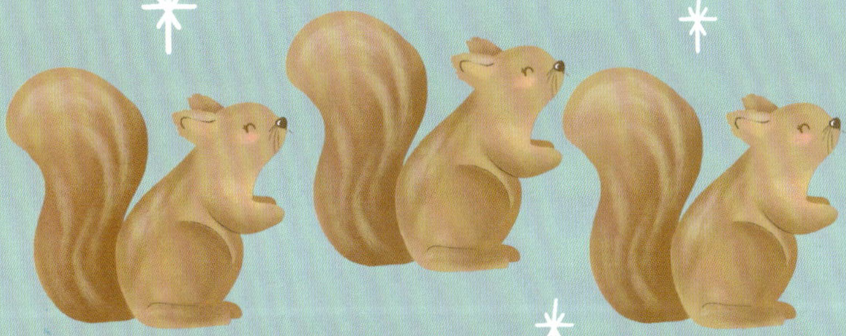

4 Owls

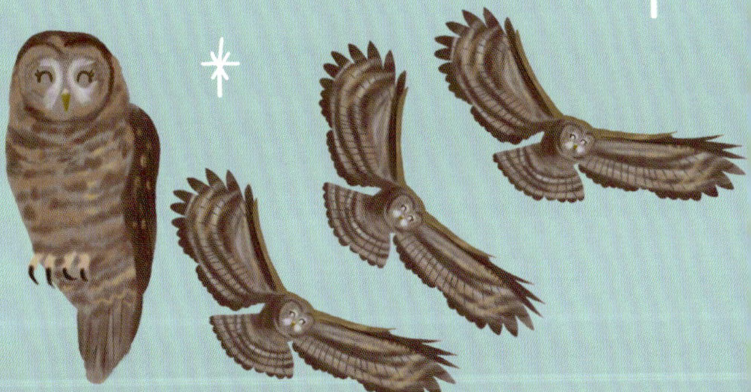

5 Brown Moths

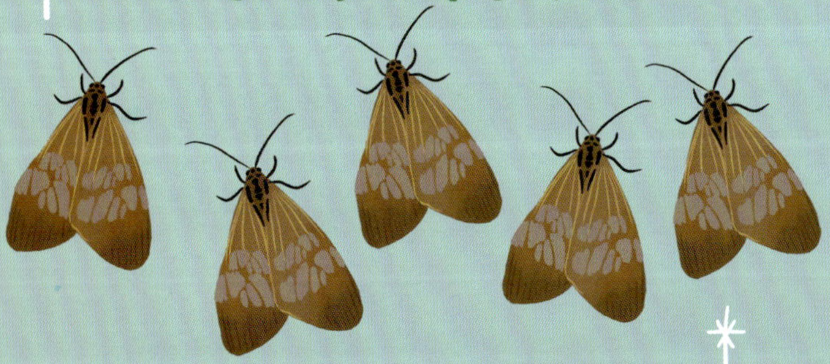

6 Blue Butterflies

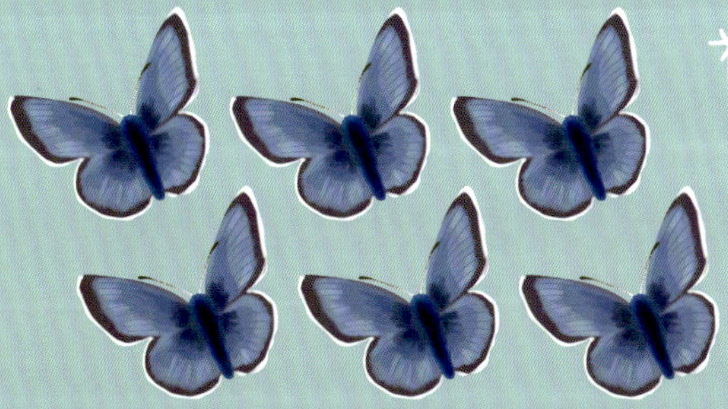

Do you ever see butterflies in your garden?

What was your favorite thing on this page?

Can you name the forest closest to you?

LAKE

Down at the water's edge can you find...

EXTRAS!

Have you seen an Otter before?

Where did you see it?

Where is your favorite lake?

MOUNTAINS

Up in the mountains can you find...

1 Bighorn Sheep

2 Tree Swallows

3 Grizzly Bears

4 Mountain Goats

5 American Pikas

6 Snowshoe Hares

EXTRAS!

Have you seen a mountain goat before?

Where did you see it?

Can you name three mountains in America?

DESERT

In the dry desert area can you find...

1 Desert Tortoise

2 American Kestrels

3 Mountain Lions

4 Giant Scorpions

5 Butterflies

6 Desert Pocket Mice

Have you seen a desert before?

Where was it?

What is the hottest place you have been to?

Did you find everything?

Canyon

Wetlands

Prairie

Waterfall

Which was your favorite page?

Forest

Lake

Mountains

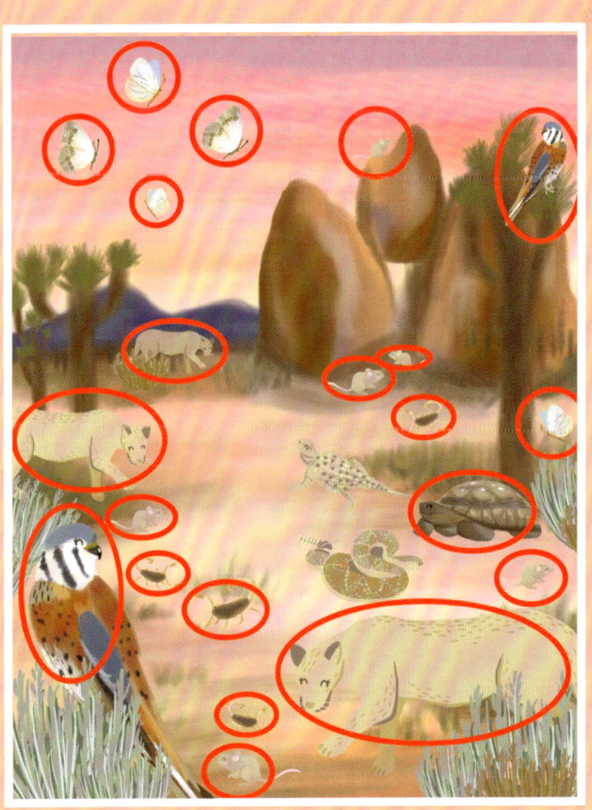

Desert

SPOT THE CREATURE

Have you spotted any of these creatures before?
Where did you see them?

These are just a few of the many animals in America.

Visit www.nps.gov for information on American national parks including the animals, birds and insects you can find in each area.

About the illustrator

Christie is an illustrator and surface pattern designer from the Dandenong Ranges, Australia. She specialises in drawing colorful illustrations and especially loves to draw flowers, birds, and cakes. Her work combines traditional drawing methods with digital techniques to create vibrant color filled designs. Christie has been professionally designing for over 10 years, with her artwork featuring on fabric, gifts and homewares, apparel, greeting cards, and now books. When she's not drawing she loves spending time reading and exploring nature.

Discover more books by Christie: